NOON

Stories and Poems
from the
Solstice Shorts Festival
2018

ARACHNE PRESS

First published in UK 2019 by Arachne Press Limited
100 Grierson Road, London SE23 1NX
www.arachnepress.com
© Arachne Press Limited
ISBNs:
print: 978-1-909208-69-8
ePub: 978-1-909208-70-4
mobi/kindle: 978-1-909208-71-1

The moral rights of the authors have been asserted.
All rights reserved. This book is sold subject to the condition that it shall not, by way of trade or otherwise, be lent, resold, hired out or otherwise circulated without the publisher's prior written consent in any form or binding or cover other than that in which it is published and without similar condition including this condition being imposed on the subsequent purchaser.
Except for short passages for review purposes no part of this publication may be reproduced, stored in a retrieval system or transmitted in any form or by any means, electronic, mechanical, photocopying, recording or otherwise, without prior written permission of Arachne Press.
Thanks to Muireann Grealy for her proofing.
Printed on wood-free paper in the UK by TJ International, Padstow.

#Noon © Su Yin Yap 2019
A Vampire at Noon © Patience Mackarness 2019
After Hours © Stuart McKenzie 2019
An Autumn Noon © Ian Grosz 2019
Angelus at Noon © Patricia McCaw 2019
Arthur Streeton Advises his Students © Mandy Macdonald 2019
By the Obelisk Sundial, Drummond Castle © Jane Aldous 2019
Farewell my Father © Anne Elizabeth Bevan 2019
Fire at Midday © Susan Cartwright-Smith 2019
High Noon © Marka Rifat 2019
I am not Beautiful at Noon © Elinor Brooks 2019
Jackdaw © Elaine Hughes 2019
Mad Dogs and English Men © Laila Sumpton 2019
Moon Jellyfish © Ness Owen 2019
Mother Hand © Karen Ankers 2019
Noon Child Unknown © Diana Powell 2019
Noon Son © Alison Lock 2019
Noon Talk © Graham Burchell 2019
On Kings and Falling © Roppotucha Greenberg 2019
On the First Calculation of the Circumference of the Earth
 © Alison Gerhard 2019
Pocket Watch © Catriona Yule 2019
precarious © Michelle Penn 2019
Still No Name © Marika Josef 2019
Sun Beats over New Orleans © Natalie Gasper 2019
Toast Crumbs © Karen Boissonneault-Gauthier 2019
Twelve o'Clock from the House © Nicholas McGaughey 2019
Under the L © Liam Hogan 2019
Unleashed © Paul Foy 2019
Up on the Roof © Lily Peters 2019
Veranda © Clare Shaw 2019
Winter Ritual © Sara Elgerot 2019
Winter Solstice © Gareth Culshaw 2019
Woman and Child © Barbara Renel 2019

NOON

Contents

Poems

Farewell my Father	Anne Elizabeth Bevan	11
I am not Beautiful at Noon	Elinor Brooks	12
Noon Talk	Graham Burchell	13
Fire at Midday	Susan Cartwright-Smith	14
By the Obelisk Sundial, Drummond Castle	Jane Aldous	15
Winter Solstice	Gareth Culshaw	16
Unleashed	Paul Foy	17
Sun Beats over New Orleans	Natalie Gasper	18
On the First Calculation of the Circumference of the Earth	Alison Gerhard	19
An Autumn Noon	Ian Grosz	20
Noon Son	Alison Lock	21
Arthur Streeton Advises his Students	Mandy Macdonald	22
Angelus at Noon	Patricia McCaw	23
Twelve o'Clock from the House	Nicholas McGaughey	24
After Hours	Stuart McKenzie	25
Moon Jellyfish	Ness Owen	26
precarious	Michelle Penn	28
Winter Ritual	Sara Elgerot	30
Pocket Watch	Catriona Yule	31
Mad Dogs and English Men	Laila Sumpton	32
Still No Name	Marika Josef	34

Stories

A Vampire at Noon	Patience Mackarness	39
Woman and Child	Barbara Renel	42
#Noon	Su Yin Yap	43
Jackdaw	Elaine Hughes	46
Toast Crumbs	Karen Boissonneault-Gauthier	49
High Noon	Marka Rifat	52
Veranda	Clare Shaw	55
Mother Hand	Karen Ankers	59
On Kings and Falling	Roppotucha Greenberg	62
Under the L	Liam Hogan	64
Noon Child Unknown	Diana Powell	69
Up on the Roof	Lily Peters	71

POEMS

Farewell My Father
Anne Elizabeth Bevan

The voice of my father reached me
From the height of the salt water spray,
Glancing the rocks with his simple accent,
More distant now than in my childhood;

I listened with jaded heart to his tune
Swaying to the familiar melody. At my feet
A dog daisy reached from beneath a bolder,
Fairer than its sisters who dusted the soft sands.

Twice I tasted a salty drop, and knowing
It was not the wild Atlantic spray
That stung my lips, I accepted the daisy
Flourishing in a barren, faded life.

A cormorant straddled the rushing water,
Feathers fluffed to the western wind
And I felt a surge of life within me
That matched the bravery of the daisy.

On the wooded hill behind me, the church
Bell toned with noontime call to prayer
And I released your thrashing spirit
To the foaming winter water.

I am not Beautiful at Noon
Elinor Brooks

At noon you think you have me
where you want me
hold me at bay
high on the tips of my own spears.

I hang like a naked light bulb
burning my prisoner's blinded eye
harangue and harry you
hot and angry.

Maddened I make you face
the white spaces of my ire
or flee into shadows
that dwindle to a dot and disappear.

I am not beautiful at noon.

But when the dark arrows of birds
pierce the hedgerows at dusk along the lanes
and you untie me from the sky
I run down the sloping fields
and launch myself out over the plain
beyond the reach of the children
and their handfuls of wet grass.

Glorious I slip beneath your horizon.

Noon Talk
Graham Burchell

is vulnerable, like December daylight.
There's not enough of it.
On this shortest of days, it shows me a slant of fine rain
in the gap between my window and the wall of laurel
opposite.
There must be a word for such a condition,
one more pewter than merely gloomy.

In Senegal where it is the same time,
There'll be no talk of precipitation, of middays
compared with metals (except perhaps gold or copper),
or of it getting dark soon. In the city of Thiès
where it is also the shortest day, who will speak of it,
sat in the shade of a giant baobab tree?

They'll have other things to laugh and cry about,
to string in sentences full of sand, pre-nasalised occlusives
and geminate consonants.

    Noon is a Cangin language of Senegal spoken in the Thiès region

Fire at Midday
Susan Cartwright-Smith

We have built our solstice bonfire,
stabbing sturdy sticks into the pliant pile
to beckon back our god
with goddess waiting patiently – is she mother now or crone?
Does she lean upon an arm or link it rapturously?
This sun has weak fingers in the midpoint of the day
and the shadows cast are short.
We test for hedgehogs,
smell the autumn smell where once there would
be snow.
The tang of blood, wet metal, leaf mould, – gone
are days when blood ran on this ground,
gone the days when my blood ran: the ripening sun
like a swelling belly;
dormancy resurfacing – the wheel once stopped in motion
creaks, as all trees breathe…
As I shield my eyes against the sun; my son moves
from my shadow.
satisfied that the fire is free of hibernation, we bird
nest up the tinder, light the beacon, pass the mead.
Around this midpoint;
I dance like fire, know freedom as the year, the day,
my self; teeter on the wave, crest the dying.
This is the dead time of the year and I,
I am alive. My old self dead,
the next life opens up – I burn away.

By the Obelisk Sundial, Drummond Castle, 1653
Jane Aldous

Picking Camomile and Thyme,
she was out in the garden,
close to the Sundial,
when she heard a kerfuffle,
up at the Castle.

All the explosions and fighting
were over by Noon.
She knew this by the way
sunlight fell across the hollows
and dials of the Obelisk.

She'd never noticed before
how the carved hearts
and triangles held such deep
shadows and that the dials
resembled deadly swords.

Soon she'd have to return
to the kitchen but for now
she watched as Noon darkened
the sandstone and wondered
what else was to come.

> Drummond Castle, Perthshire,
> was sacked by Oliver Cromwell in 1653

Winter Solstice
Gareth Culshaw

When the earth has become a jug
and tilts away the summer's sun
I'm left with shadows and owls.

Winter hibernates trees, blows
away seeds, falls down chimney
pots. Darkness stretches out,

holds back the light. I walk into
tunnels, squeeze my way through
the weather. There's an open door

in the sky allows winds to brush
away what I know, have grown.
The sun hauls itself to the parapets

and gables, holds the towns and cities
in its weakest noon. Then curtains
close before I'm home and a light bulb

turns my ceiling to a summer sky.

Unleashed
Paul Foy

Flames on windscreens; deluge of light unleashed.
Tributaries of sunshine splash and snap against
side street walls, roaming down stone worn stairways
to deep rooted shadows, yappy dogs to an old hound.
A solitary shaft slaps windows, challenging traffic,
racing quick glances: A cocktail is shaken in tinted trails;
here, a glint off a razor as a neck is shorn
in a Turkish barber's shop; in a flower shop,
petals reach out, clear their throats;
a floor above hunched shoulders in a betting shop, a girl sings
through the mercury chimes, her open apartment window
a momentary mirror reflecting light casting shadows in a cave;
all sounds but this harmony are silenced.
I am owned by this commonality:
the clash of cloud, sun, metallic blue sky;
owned by the race through the crowd,
the steady plod of feet and pushchair wheels on pavement slabs.
A boy rattles a collection tin.
Mistress of Finesse, of Fickleness, take notice,
here is our sadness and our happiness –
autumn leaves in a puddle when the rain has stopped,
the bells chime, and the sun pushed through.
Strange. There are no trees here.

Sun Beats over New Orleans
Natalie Gasper

I took a stroll past Jackson Square
today, just as the out-of-tune bell
began to mark the luncheon hour.
The first chime rang out as two
young lovers stole a kiss beneath
the low hanging branches of a vibrant
oak tree. Three marked the horse-drawn
carriages as they clip-clopped and rolled
down Decatur Street. Four tourists ambled
by with their fresh *beignets* as the fifth
bell sounded. With the sixth chime
came a soft breeze off the Mississippi
River, the only relief from this seven
day streak of midday July heat. Eight
artists stationed by the wrought-iron
fence made their final marks on bright
cityscapes as the bell sang out, striking
its ninth peal. A flutter of wings drew
my eyes to the sky, as ten mourning
doves made their daily rounds above
Andrew Jackson, his hat forever tipped
to everyone who passes, his mount reared
up to greet the day. At the eleventh bell,
the sun, peeking out from billowy white
clouds, cast shadows scarcely large enough
for field mice. High-noon came at last,
with a final, echoing clang
expanding out across the square.

On the First Calculation of the Circumference of the Earth
Alison Gerhard

Such luck,
to look down a well at noon
and think
'That's funny...'

More people knew the world was round
then we ever gave them credit for.
Columbus was an ass
in kindergarten classes,
when we thought of tipping edges
and some mystery beyond.

Archimedes got his eureka in a bathtub
and his promises to move
the very ground we stand on.

Eratosthenes got a stick and three camels
and found the size of everything there was to know.

(46,100 km
as the earth turns)

An Autumn Noon
Ian Grosz

In the half-done day
before afternoon's pull,
    a pause,
as the sun finds its balance
between extremes.

Darkness seems distant
as sunlight, gathered
in a gaze drawn upward,
recalls the long summer song,
singing in the blaze
of its midday,

    but waits
in the shrunken shadows
of the leaf-bare trees
that live remembering
the deep dark of winter
    to come.

Noon Son
Alison Lock
(for George)

The opal eyes of dawn had long since opened when I first saw you.
As clocks ticked on, they digitised your entry, the exit
from my body marked me as calendar.

From that time on, our counting days began with breaks
at midnight and beyond. You are my noon son, the age I was
when I had you at Pluto's rising moon.

So, we are balanced on the scales of time, noon boy and I, astride
the line of the meridian, a palindrome
where shadows fade, double 'o's no longer link, where the sun

becomes a moon-bow in the winter's sky, laid horizontal
to the earth, but in good time our hemispheres will separate
and then we'll be the noon, the dusk, the night, the dawn.

Arthur Streeton Advises his Students
Mandy Macdonald

No, none of that flat, transparent light!
Your light needs to slant, scatter, explode
in loose, fierce brushstrokes, white-hot
blades fallen off the sun
to crash-land among your gum trees,
smash the vertical design.

Think of those skeleton trunks as maenads –
you know the myth, don't you? Bacchus
and his dancers – sinewy, silvery,
improbably upright;
the maddening thyrsus wand
a shaken gesture of leaves high up,
thick flicks of grey-white paint
edged with sun, praising the light,
its cruelty.

Whatever pigments you use,
think of everything
as white. If there is water in these pictures,
put no blue in it. Make it a quicksilver snake.
The grass between trees, a sheet of pale beaten gold.

Out here
it is everlasting, violent noon.

Angelus at Noon
Patricia McCaw

Then
The midday bell is mournful, the girl kneels
all fourteen stations of the cross, knees speared
on gravel spread by nuns. She wants to feel
His pain, the Passion of two thousand years ago.
A crucifix stabs her palm, blood trickles to her socks.

Now
A bell peals three times each day, an angel declares
Mary's sexless impregnation. The Angelus sounds
at noon on Radio Eireann, still a long-time favourite.
The Taoiseach listens, his husband bows his head,
women stop to ponder their new rights at conception.

A labourer spreads silage,
a landlady pours a Guinness.
All pause in the bell's after-silence,
knowing that Grace has arrived at last.

Twelve o'Clock from the House
Nicholas McGaughey

Twelve o'clock from the house!
Down to The Arms…
Some of the boys'd sneak food in…
Everyone red and
Rocking like a shanty. He,
Stout as the anthem, stood
On the green battlefield
Of two nations at war.

No talk 'til the half!

Twelve o'clock from the house,
We follow to his flowers
A legend that under
The coloured window
Is new remembered.
The Arms feel empty
And the snug is black
Crammed with tales and titbits
And a place at the bar never taken.

After Hours
Stuart McKenzie

We roll out of the club at noon –
the closest place to hell I'd ever been
but I'd still stayed anyway, now
emerging to that lost part of the day
we hoped we'd see, but it's brief.

Sunday morning strollers are still out
as I count down on my fingers
the hours I have
to get my head together
before work the next day.

I swear I'm still rushing
as I struggle with euphoria –
here to spread love all over the world,
gonna kiss the sky, you've never been so high
before we realise
we haven't quite made it
over noon's threshold
and I get to plunder
the day for all its worth.

Moon Jellyfish
Ness Owen

Half the day is gone
our words evaporate
into the warm silence
of the midday sun.
We listen to the
bladder-wrack crunch
step carefully over the
beached jellyfish lulled
by the warm currents.
You want to paddle
and have to steady
yourself on my arm
it's easy to forget your
age as our footprints
disappear into the wet
sand. Your feet half
the size of mine now
but I always felt bigger
even when I was small.
I fill the silence with
stories of beach days
with my friends the
jellyfish we swam
through but only one
of us was stung. Moon
jellyfish glow at night.
You don't ask why.

My thirst to know won't
end but why should we
be the same? You don't
remember the jellyfish
stories or letting me go
out on the bike with no
brakes but you remember
the girl taken by the wave
and the mother who
couldn't lock doors in
case one day her little
girl would find her way
home.

precarious
Michelle Penn

        it is exactly noon   i am standing

at the black corner of california

    and the edge of the world

the bay's chill burnishing my cheeks

       it could be any season   people joke

    that there *are* four   earthquakes

floods fires and construction   but we

    really know only this one   its warm-

bite water weighting the air

    or drowning the gutters

making these hills slick as lies   why

       did people choose to live here

      building matchstick victorians

at the place where the ground shoved

    its guts toward the sky   on this black corner

of california and the edge of life   in this never-

        one-thing-or-the-other weather   up

    the slope from our flat with its brick

that will collapse the next time the earth

    wrenches   walking is irrelevant   i have

                always been here

Winter Ritual
Sara Elgerot

At noon

this far north

in the grip of winter

Humankind comes out en masse
for the brief quivering of the sun.

We savour it

drink it

ritually.

As to will its existence

for the next day
and the next.

Doubting –
but with hope –

for the Sun
to bless us

yet again.

Pocket Watch
Catriona Yule

I serve lunch in the workshop:
a bunch of glistening cherries, hunk
of Gruyère cheese, some flat bread,
water, and Rioja for grandfather.

The old man pecks as he grafts:
graphite smear on a cheek bone,
eyelids sweat-soaked as stubby
fingers grapple with a toothpick.

I pass him a rag over the bench,
silenced by the concentration
which fixes his face in a grimace,
and watch the tiny spring cajoled
into place,

animating the dial.

Mad Dogs and English Men
Laila Sumpton

Tristan chases his tail,
Eustacia snarls at water,
no one has seen Agamemnon
and Hyacinth is on heat.

We're all rather busy,
for this is our time–
when we dare to pinken.
When we tread your sacred climbs,
assess your dozing towns
and groom flagging maharajahs
till they canter to bugle and drum.

When you wake,
our plan will be done:
your feet will carry ours
to lands ripe for draining,
leaving us more time for croquet,
poetry and meandering letters home.

You'll find you have actually agreed
to till, plant and ship all you have
back to our rainy parlours
anxiously awaiting tea.

We muddle gin and straighten the map
of a plot you've never realised.
We'll use this midday sun
to rename mountains, reappoint rivers
and decide the exact ratio
of how many weavers
need broken thumbs
for our mills back home
to bloom.

We plan at the peak of the sun
whilst ayahs fan our brows
and the cook sweats into
a large Victoria sponge
before carving up a chicken
for all our errant hounds.

Still No Name
Marika Josef

Church clock strikes on a barren eave.
He's got spikes to match those of the dry brush. He smokes.
Draped below, the reckoning stretches ahead, dusty, earthy.
It burns bright with the soot in his eyes. It strikes.

Church clock strikes on a barren heath.
He's counted every stitch on every mistake he's made, tender as
Ancestral quilt-threads. Stripped bare as bark, bitten raw as
Dry whiskey screams. Another patient. It strikes.

Church clock strikes on barren leaves.
He squints against the bald sun of high noon, to hold the
Sight firm or it'll crumble to the touch. When a stranger comes to
Town, night and day cannot agree on what favours to grant the
Time. It stri–stutters.

Grinds.

Church clock strikes.
And still he is only halfway.

He knows how these stories end, as they must. Old pulp tales:
A past wrong put right.
An enigma in bullet-hole braille.
Judge, jury, and a first and final home in the ground,
Forgotten but for
Hungry jackals screaming in the drought.

He won't return.

But until the chimes suffocate:
He will have beaten the sun to its highest point.
He will have followed the lines in his hands.

And then:
Then, he will take the step.

A creak rends country silence. A suggestion
Unspools.

He is ready.

By noontime, he will be.

STORIES

A Vampire at Noon
Patience Mackarness

That summer half-term in Palma de Mallorca, both our kids were in a vampire phase.

Lucy, just sixteen, was obsessed by the Twilight Saga, with its repressed sexuality, Robert Pattinson's pale face and beautiful haunted eyes. Jack, aged nine, preferred the vampire bat side of things: transformation, superpowers, gory fangs.

Apparently it was one of the hottest Junes on record. Our apartment had no air conditioning, was surrounded by taller buildings and faced south, so we sweated all night and headed out each morning to seek shade and sea breezes. As we processed down the baking *avenida* with our beach gear, coolbag, sunscreen and parasols, Gerald warbled, 'Mad dogs and Englishmen go out in the midday sun' with a Noël Coward lilt, which was his way of reminding me how badly I had screwed up with my choice of apartment. Lucy and Jack were unfazed; they slept well in spite of the heat, and the beach suited them perfectly. Most days we were there by ten a.m., and spent our time in and out of the sea, fetching ice-creams and drinks, reading, snorkelling, having goes on banana-boats. We always ate lunch at the same restaurant, which had a flame tree growing in the centre of its shady courtyard.

It was under the flame tree that we got talking about the finer points of vampirism. Jack said, 'You know how you can tell a vampire's a vampire because it doesn't cast a shadow?'

Lucy said in her weary I-know-it-all-because-I'm-sixteen way, 'Of course, squirt, who doesn't?'

'But if the sun's right overhead, like now, *no-one* casts a shadow, do they? So if a vampire was here, we wouldn't know.'

Lucy's eyes flickered for a moment, but she said with a

contemptuous laugh, 'Of course we'd know, because as soon as the sun hit him, he'd melt.'

'Suppose he had protection?' Jack persisted. 'A long cloak. Big gloves. A big hat.'

Gerald, who was a teacher and always turned conversations in an educational direction if he could, began to explain about cloth not giving total protection from UV rays, but then the calamari and chips arrived, and we were busy for some time. It was during dessert that Jack looked up from his Knickerbocker Glory and cried, 'There's a vampire! See him?'

Across the road, under a plane tree, a huge gleaming motorcycle had just pulled up. The rider swung his leg over the back of the bike and moved into a patch of sunlight. He was tall, and in spite of the forty-degree temperature was wearing serious biker kit: full-face helmet, black leathers, boots with silver buckles, big black gauntlets. He cast no shadow.

Lucy and Jack stared at him, wide-eyed. Gerald, who had once owned a 250 cc Suzuki and had never quite got over missing it, eyed the shiny monster bike with desire. I thought what a stupid poser the man was.

A girl who had been sitting at a table in the corner of the courtyard then got up and walked past us towards the entrance gateway. I don't know why we hadn't noticed her before – perhaps Gerald had, and pretended not to – because she was wearing something short and white and diaphanous, more like a negligée than a sun dress, and her skin had the kind of paleness you'd really have to work hard at, in Mallorca in one of the hottest Junes on record. She walked across the road to the motorcyclist, who stood at least a foot taller. I thought he would remove his helmet and embrace her, but instead he turned back to the bike, straddled it and waited, without looking round. The girl climbed on, gracefully side-saddle, and put her white hands on his waist. He kicked the motorcycle into life, pushed off from the kerb and they were away, with a deep virile thrumming like a bass-note among the street sounds that hot afternoon. White fabric fluttered around white legs as they turned the corner.

Watching my family watching them disappear, I knew without a wisp of doubt what was going on in the mind of each. Lucy was feeling in her own fingertips the smoothness of the black leather, the lean male flanks underneath. Jack was picturing the whole ensemble gathering itself in a mid-air blur, morphing into something with huge beating wings. Gerald's breathless attention, I understood with relief and a dash of disappointment, was focused not on the white thighs of the passenger but on the black-and-chrome beast beneath them.

And I? I ordered another *Chocolate con Churros*, with extra cream.

Woman and Child
Barbara Renel

Noontime. The top of the pendulum. A moment of suspension between inspiration, exhalation, rise and fall. A moment of uncertainty.

She waits, unsure which path to take. Stillness.

She hears voices on the wind, laughing, and she looks back. In the distance a figure. No, two. A woman, a child following. She watches as the child catches up with the woman and disappears inside her. The woman approaches. Her belly is swollen.

Why are you waiting?

I don't know which path to take.

We can walk together.

The child climbs out of the woman and runs ahead, sure of the way.

#Noon
Su Yin Yap

Noon flicked through her Instagram feed, her French manicured nails tap-tapping on the screen. #Sunrise, #sunset, #gratitude, #wonderofnature – it made her want to puke. Everybody wanted a selfie with Sunrise or Sunset, but what about *her?* What was wrong with Noon? Noon was the moment at which Sun was at the peak of her powers, the midway point in the day, the half way line between one midnight and the next, but people had no appreciation for the classics these days. They were only interested in the big names. Where were *her* Insta followers? The curse of the middle child, she thought – always overlooked.

Sunset was insufferable about her follower numbers; her air of superiority wafted around her like expensive perfume. She took every opportunity to pontificate to her younger sisters about *building a fan base*, her *personal brand, search engine optimization*. Noon always felt a bit panicky listening to this marketing speak; she didn't know what these phrases meant, much less how to action them. Sunrise, however, affected a glazed-over boredom during these impromptu lectures, and barely looked up from watching YouTube clips of ninja cats and hilarious dog fails. Her older sister's graphs and pie charts were only for suits, and as for Facebook followers – that was just embarrassing. Everyone knew it was only for old people. For Sunrise, social media was like breathing, and she didn't consider her oldest sister to be any real threat. After all, she had a 98% approval rating for doing little more than bending into sun salutations wearing tight lycra, making kale smoothies, or occasionally smashing an avocado onto sourdough – #wellness, #cleanliving. Her youth was bewildering to Noon. She even knew how to use the storyboard function on Insta, for Christ's sake.

Well, this Winter Solstice, Noon was going to upstage them both. This was her time.

Her minion crouched at her feet, filing and buffing her hooves, trying to get down to the level of pink skin well hidden under the layers of grey hide. It was expensive and time consuming work, this sunny natural look. She couldn't just slap on some smoky eyeliner like Sunset and look all moody; no, she had to work hard for this sun-kissed look. Spray tan once a week, all over body scrubs to avoid patchiness, dry body brushing to keep the cellulite at bay. As for the contouring, that Kardashi-butts one had a lot to answer for. And who knew there were that many shades on the tan to beige spectrum? She was sick of bloody taupe, nude, mushroom – she wanted colour! To go wild with the new Chanel eye liner in Aqua, paint her toenails in Cherry Pop, dye her hair acid pink. Did her sisters ever think of that? No, they did not, spin-dizzy on their fame and billion hashtag mentions.

Well, this would show them. Now smoothly hooved, she smiled to herself in anticipation, the hum of her secret plan vibrating in her belly. She reached for the tray of samples on the chaise-longue beside her, filled with rhinestones and Swarovskis, running her fingers through their glorious technicolour. She felt strangely soothed by the sound, reminding her as it did of small stones on the shoreline being bathed by the sea. *Like a rhinestone cowboy,* she hummed, *Riding out on a horse in a star-spangled rodeo...* it was certainly going to be spangled, that's for sure.

The Newgrange crowd would hate it. The ones who drove out to some god-forsaken place in rural Ireland, and queued up in the dark and drizzle on Winter Solstice, just to see Sunrise flooding the chamber of the megalithic tomb. Or something equally snoresome as that. It was her sister's party piece. She had never paid much attention to it, to be honest. Full of the Gore-tex brigade, as she called them, the Wholesomes, who earnestly filled their Thermos flasks with Fairtrade coffee, and packed enough ginger nut biscuits to share. They probably used words like *blessed*, *humbling*, and *inspirational* to describe it. Was there anything that made her want to shoot herself in the face faster than the Gore-tex brigade? Well, she would show them *inspirational*. They would be appalled by the level of bling she had in mind for this noon. She would blow the roof off their *blessed* tomb!

Oh, Noon had plans, big plans. This noon-time showdown would go down in history. Like a static solar firework show, she was going to light up the sky in a halo of jewel tones – ruby red, emerald green, blue sapphire. It would be like one of those child's kaleidoscopes where the tiniest twist of a wrist made colourful shapes burst into pattern after pattern. She would make sure that there was just enough time for people to get their selfies – oh yes, they would get their bloody selfies. *And there had better be a #noon trending on Twitter after it*, she thought.

She felt dizzy with the anticipation of it all. Steady yourself, Noon, she thought, don't get too excited. This had to be just right. Standing in front of her wardrobe, she took out her rhinestone-encrusted playsuit. It flashed and glinted in the light, a slithery sliver of colour amid a sea of neutrals.

Showtime!

Jackdaw
Elaine Hughes

Now the wind had dropped to a low moan.

All night she had lain awake. Sadness stabbing her heart. The moon was no comfort. Its blank face staring through thin curtains, sweeping silver beams into the corners of her empty nest.

Later, in the pearl light, cats clamoured. Whipping cruel tails into her eyes. The tabby padding her face. Green eyes narrowing as the pad became a prickle and then a cruel spike to her cheek.

She sighed and spooned chunks into silver bowls. They grunted and gorged, bells tinkling. The big tabby one and the little black one.

Settling herself on the sofa – TV faces blinked behind cold glass. Her gaze lifted and swept the line of photographs. A lump rose like a tired sun into the hill of her throat.

But now it was noon. She opened the front door. Rain had washed the garden. Silver beads danced on orange nasturtiums. A spider's web picked out in diamonds clung to the gate. The towering slate heaps glittered in sunlight. Noon – the empty pages of the day opened out – ready for ink and action.

She set about hauling sheets up the steps to the line. A sea of children's voices rose in waves from Penybryn School. A small sadness tried to creep up – but she willed it down. It seemed only last week that her boy had ambled down the slate steps to Penybryn. The man with the skinny dogs from number 42 waved. She waved back and the quarry boom rolled out like a cannon ball across the sky.

It was after the silence that she became aware of the jackdaws. At this time of year she swept up their discarded sticks, strange blue fluff and string. Once, a jackdaw had even dropped an old meat bone on her head at the washing line.

She was used to their chatter echoing in the chimney breast. Congregating above – swooping back and forth on the slated roof. An unkindness of ravens, a scold of jays – a clattering of jackdaws. The clattering had become a high pitched shrieking now. She shivered, as the sun disappeared.

Inside, the house seemed to be holding its breath. Damp soot in her nostrils, the sofa hazy in a mist of grime. She froze. A small ball of energy bristled, drawing her to the open kitchen door. And there he was. His eyes were the brightest blue periwinkles, intelligent, penetrating. Cocking his head and quivering, he sized her up. He was no little chick, he was a teenager, a gawky fledgling. A spiky plume stuck up from his head, as if he had applied hair gel that very morning before his arrival down the chimney. She stifled a chuckle.

A tabby face appeared at the window. She bolted the back door. The black one was asleep upstairs on her bed. She crept forward to the sound of frantic fluttering. He was charging at the kitchen cupboards. He managed a shaky lift off, wings half unfurled, only to crash downwards and wobble across the tiled floor. After a few more attempts, he skittered into a corner next to the washing machine and stared at her with his bright blue eyes. 'Well my boy, what now?' she said. He teetered over to the cat bowl and pecked. A frantic yowling started up from the window, and she drew down the blind with a 'Sorry, Puss'.

A storm was brewing and fat raindrops lashed the window. He tottered after her. His parents were cawing down the echoing chimney in despair. She called up – 'I'll do my best, I promise.' But the doleful cries continued.

Unperturbed, he staggered around the room. A large mirror became a focus of great interest. He wobbled up to the glass and let out a long thin caaaaw. A mournful call echoed back from the chimney, but he carried on staring into the mirror. With another high pitched caw he started pecking at his reflection. She felt a gust of laughter roll out of her throat. Startled, he fluttered his wings and hopped from foot to foot.

She smiled as he preened himself in the mirror and twitched his head from side to side. All that evening long, he entertained her. Swooping up on top of the piano, and strutting along the black and white keys. Fluttering his wings and attempting several take offs on top of the sideboard and down again as she applauded. He stared at her in the glow of the dying firelight. 'Well 'ol blue eyes, you have really entertained me tonight,' she said. He jittered a little jig across the hearth in response, and she roared with laughter.

The next morning she carried him outside. The birds were wheeling overhead. Thick black lines on the rooftops of the bungalows across the road. The sky was a cobalt blue and one lone cloud scudded across the slate tops, a white sail cut free from a mast. His feathers were warm, and his heart beat against her cupped palms. He didn't struggle, his eyes blue and patient and unblinking. 'Thank you,' she whispered. She spread her palms. He waited a while. Urgent cawing sounded from the black lines on the rooftops. His first attempt sent him flailing into the fuchsia bush. It took him three attempts to a loud raucous cawing. A black arc reeled across the sky as he flew in their escort. He clung to the wall of a garage. Two loud urgent cries encouraged him up to the roof. He fluttered his way up to join them and the sky and rooftops burst into a jubilant jackdaw celebration. 'It takes a whole community to raise a child,' she thought.

And now it was noon. Sunlight glittered on the slate heaps, and the quarry boom rolled out like a cannon ball across the sky.

Toast Crumbs
Karen Boissonneault-Gauthier

(*Location:* Porch)

I listen for a loud clack from the back door of my Grandpa's house. I'm rewarded with a resounding slam because I've left open the front parlour window. It makes this amazing air vacuum, so Grandpa's screen door bangs hard to a close… an open… and another close. 'Don't slam de-door!' he yells at me, thinking I've just come inside.

We've now comfortably deposited ourselves in plastic chairs on the front porch. It's raining this morning and it's the kind of rain shower which brings fat worms slithering onto the cement sidewalk. I'll be picking them up later. 'Where does rain came from?' I ask him. He looks stiffly at me and tells me it's God crying. So I ask him, 'Was it something I've done?'
'You slammed de-damn-door!' is his answer.

He'll usually sit here, feeding peanuts to squirrels or rolling cigarettes. He's always got his old police scanner at his feet, turned on and tuned in to the station he once worked for. I ask him why he likes it here on the porch… killing time. He just shrugs. The scanner buzzes to life, broadcasting some new emergency. At least someone is up to no good. I decide to go pick worms.

(*Location:* Swing)

We walk down to the park at the end of our street because it has stopped raining. I like to swing and kick sand. I kick sand to see just how far I can make it spray. It disperses and fans out like pigeon feed from clenched fists. Grandpa gives me pushes on the swing, but never those 'underdogs'. He tells me he's too old to run under my butt.

His hands are meaty, intimidating even… taking up the whole small space of my back. I hope my hands will mature one day and get large like his. He nicknamed them *War Hands*. I bet Grandpa can hold a lot of birdseed, but in his day, he used them for throwing grenades and later wielding a Billy Club. I hope there's still some fight left in 'em.

I check on him mid-swing while arching my back and stretching out my legs. I spot him upside down on my upswing, taking a drag of one of his newly rolled cigarettes. This morning, on the porch, he let me lick the rolling papers to seal the tobacco. He looks a bit lost. I find myself drifting backwards into a fog of his exhaled smoke.

I guess he used to do this kind of thing with my Dad, but since the porch police scanner made its big announcement, it's just the two of us. I could be wrong about him being lost. Maybe he's trying to remember my Dad and Grandma as they drove away together. I'm swinging to forget.

(*Location:* Table)

I wonder about a grown man who's got a lace cloth on his kitchen table. It traps toast crumbs and I really hate cleaning de-damn-things. *War Hands* seem out their element, stroking and smoothing a big lace doily. They look so brawny and it looks too delicate to withstand such a touch. He says his wife liked lace and he loved her; so the doily cloth stays.

By noon he's seated at the table, working on his crossword puzzle while I go over my homework. Steam from his hot tea distracts me and more cigarette smoke hypnotically twirls before disappearing towards the ceiling. If he does speak to me, it's while I'm sharpening our lead pencils, telling me to get the lead out. Alphabet letters become confined in crossword squares like crumbs get trapped in lace. Somehow, we all get stuck in a rut.

I stare down at my Grandma's cloth and set myself to task, pecking away at the imprisoned toast crumbs and fresh pencil shavings ensnared within its ornamental weave. I have a memory of her kissing my Dad on the cheek as he'd breeze into this house and with me in tow, for every Sunday lunch. The aroma of roasted turkey permeated the house, teasing my senses with all her hard work. This makes me consider closing the front parlour window once in a while, to stop giving God a reason to cry.

I think she'd like that.

High Noon
Marka Rifat

'Howdy pardner.'

'Howdy, Dan.'

They tipped back their Stetsons and gazed sternly into the distance.

'Any action on the High Sierra?'

'Naw, naeb'dy wiz ... Ah mean nope, Ah was scoutin' on the ridge after breakfast and there was nae loose steer north or south, Danny.'

'Head of cattle's gotta be somewhere, Connor, an' rustlin's a dirty business.'

'Them dang rustlers'll get what's comin' tae them. Yessiree. Ah'll make sure o' that today, Dan.'

The two cowboys nodded with grim conviction. It was going to be a tough day, but they would face down those ornery no-good desperados and they would beat 'em. Connor silently passed a treacle toffee to Danny. It was the closest to chewing tobacco Connor could find in Uncle Dod's sweetie tin, and the whole gang agreed it was brilliant for making black spitballs. It was important to impress the gang.

'Reckon we need some Sarsaparilla. Sun's getting high in the sky.'

They set off for the Dry Gulch Saloon, known to others as McNab's Shop'n'save, their progress slowed by practising their swagger and testing out their quick-draw techniques.

Cans of cola in their pockets, they negotiated the single carriageway of Skull River Pass, daringly crossing while the green man was flashing, and avoided a tribe of marauding Sioux warriors in the guise of shrieking girls from the high school returning from their swimming lesson.

They paused outside the Thistle Tavern and crouched close to the ground.

'These are fresh today, Connor.'

'Darn tootin'. Looks like the Left Hand Gang, maybe twelve of the varmints.'

The boys re-counted the cigarette stubs on the pavement.

'Yup, reckon a good twelve, and they ain't gonna git far.'

They reached the swings and climbing frame of Cowhide City and joined the gang. Connor shared out the treacle toffees, then tactics, weaponry and terrain were discussed. The ceremonial handover had just begun when Connor was hauled backwards by a meaty hand clamped onto the back of his collar.

'Aagh! We've been ambushed!'

He wriggled to face the dang-blastit enemy who'd dared to sneak up on his big day. The hand belonged to his mother. She was breathing fast and redder than a prairie sunset.

'Connor! Christ, Ah've been looking everywhere. You canna just bugger aff. The Social wifie's coming the morn and she's got tae see baith o' us.'

She winced, pressed her free hand into the folds of fat over her ribs, and pushed her face into his. He smelled beer.

'Christ, ye've gied me a seizure.' She hauled herself upright. She glared at the little boys in their checked shirts and cardboard hats. 'Piss aff ye wee nutters.'

She yanked him by his skinny arm back in the direction of their flat.

'But Ma, I canna go back yet, it's my big day, please! I've waited ages! Please, dinna make me.'

She was wheezing by the time they reached the Thistle and sat heavily on a beer crate by the back door. Connor glowered and swayed with rage. Bubbles of snot covered his top lip. He drew his Colt from the elasticated waistband of his jeans and aimed it between her eyes. The late morning light caught the peeling silver paint on the gun barrel.

'Whit?'

'It's. My. Turn. For. Sheriff. Today. Ah waited ages for my turn. It's nearly high noon and Ah'm in charge of rounding up the rustlers and leading the shoot-outs and *everything*. I've worked it all out, it's gonnna be brilliant, best ever. Let me go or Ah'll shoot.'

She looked at his fierce little face and for once didn't see his bastard father, and all the misery he'd brought, but a boy who could maybe have a chance to make something of his life. She started to cry. Connor kept his gun trained on her, then she mumbled 'Sorry' and opened her arms. The smokers who had been watching the scene turned away and Connor bent down. She cried into his shoulder and squeezed him tight.

'It's ok Ma, stop greeting.'

Eventually she stopped. She wiped her face on her sleeve and sighed.

'Are you really in charge today? The big boss?'

Connor looked through the grubby windows of the Thistle to the clock over the bar. 'Not any more. It's five past high noon. I've missed my turn.'

He re-holstered his Colt and adjusted his Stetson.

'C'mon cowboy. The Social wifie'll be chappin' at the door.'

They walked in silence to the corner of their road. The Family Support Worker's car was parked outside their block.

She patted his bony shoulder. 'Ah'm sorry about your big day, son. You'll be sheriff next time.'

He shook his head. 'You have to wait your turn. That's how it goes.'

'But what if you were, em, kidnapped by, ye ken, whatsits, Comanches–'

'Well, maybe if they tied me up and tortured me for days and days–'

The Family Support Worker was standing on the pavement tapping her watch.

'We'll see Mrs Iron Breeks first, Connor, then we'll plan your escape from the Injuns.'

Connor was already standing proud in the dusty main street of Cowhide City, the townsfolk clapping and the six-pointed star of authority blazing on his chest in the noonday sun.

Veranda
Clare Shaw

The food was ready in the kitchen, shrouded like a body by a large white cloth. All was in order. I stepped out onto the patio and tilted my head to study the sky where the grey haze was thinning and the sun was creeping through the gauze of cloud. You followed me out, grinning.

'It's midday, we can have a drink now.'

'Don't say noon, as if it's some sort of signal to get drunk. As if you've been waiting all morning to get a beer down your throat. Noon, noon, noon.' Salt water surged up and my throat tightened. It was the tension of entertaining, the worry that the food would be burnt and guests disappointed. It was the memory of noon. It was much later that I remembered he had said midday. But it was the same thing, wasn't it?

The first time, I am on the veranda leaping off the wooden boards onto the grass a few inches below. I hear my mother coming and I run behind the box hedge, panting too loudly. She does not hear.

'Gin and tonic please, Wilson. I've been needing one all morning. Still, it's noon now.'

What is it about noon that requires this special drink? I stay behind the hedge until my mother cries and is led away by my father. It is dusk.

The last time, I am on the veranda playing with my doll, Lucy. She has wavy blonde hair and a smiling porcelain face and she is dressed in a burgundy velvet dress and I am sitting her down on the oak floor in front of my tiny china tea set. It smells of polish and my father's pipe tobacco down here. I am lost enough in pretend to be almost happy. The grandfather clock in the drawing room nearby begins its steady clang of twelve. Then my mother arrives.

'Noon at last, make me a martini, Wilson.'

I try and melt into the wooden slats, for I have a habit of getting under her feet and I have no idea how I manage that. I can be pressed up against the wall, yards from her shoes and yet still I am under her feet or simply getting on her nerves. I am where I am not meant to be, I am in the way. My mother strolls towards the edge of the veranda and looks down to the gardens below with their roses and neatly clipped hedges, gardens which are out of bounds to me. Wilson passes her the glass, she drinks it quickly and without speaking holds the glass out for it to be refilled with the magic potion. I crawl along the floor and almost make it to the door when I hear the clip clip of footsteps and I dive behind the divan where I cannot be seen.

A woman arrives and then my father with another man. There is laughter and it gets merrier as the glasses clink and the corks pop. This sounds like happiness. Their chatter drones on, something about our neighbour, Lady Calderwood, followed by a cackle of bitter laughter. Then the men talking of rounds of golf and tennis tournaments while the women's laughter turns to high-pitched squeals like monkeys in a zoo. Then words with no meaning, sentences which slur and I cannot follow. Then 'Alice'. My name. I curl up to make myself smaller in my place behind the divan.

'Send her away to school,' the man says gruffly. 'I went at seven.'

'Yes, you're right. That's the answer.'

But what is the question? I will come out from my hiding place and demand that I am not sent away to school. But I feel a warm trickle between my legs and I am trapped.

'She's driven me to drink.'

There is a murmur of laughter. It is so hard to tell why some things are funny. They hear my sobs and I am dragged out and sent to my room. The following week a trunk is packed. I leave at noon. My mother is not there to wave me off. She has other things to do.

It is the gym mistress who notices the bruises. 'You've been in the wars,' she announces. But nobody asks the right questions. I come from a very good family.

'Hey,' you said. 'What have you got against noon?'

'I don't know. It's not one thing or another. It isn't morning, it isn't afternoon.' It's a word that means entitled, and hurt.

'Who says noon anyway,' you said. 'It's your privileged background coming to the fore again.'

'It depends what you mean by privileged.'

The doorbell rang and I let in Sally with the cake. She opened the box to show me the white icing with the chocolate piped message – Happy 80th Birthday to a Wonderful Mother.

'I'd better go and collect her,' you said.

Sally took the cloth off the food and made a space for the cake in the middle of the feast. I wanted to gouge out the icing letters and punch my fist into it. I wanted to throw it at her as soon as she arrived. But I was much too well brought up for that.

'Thank you so much, Sally,' I said, then stared across the garden wondering where I could hide.

Mother Hand
Karen Ankers

I'm late for work, as usual. Running round looking for my keys, as usual – how do they always end up down the back of the sofa? I run into the kitchen to grab some fruit to take with me, glance up at the old, scratched clock to check the time, and that's when I notice. The little hand is missing.

The big hand is almost at eleven. I watch, impatiently, to see if the little hand will peep out from behind it, but it doesn't. First thought. Find an alternative method of time-watching. Where's my phone? At the bottom of my bag. Of course it is. 11.55. Next thought. She'll be lonely.

Where did that come from? I watch the big hand, the mother hand, and I know she'll just keep going, visiting each number before she moves on. She won't even notice her child is gone. Will she?

No one noticed any change in me when you left. I made sure of that. I carried on, did all the usual things. I went to work, cleaned the house. Any gaps in my greyscaled soul were covered each morning with bright clothes and makeup. Caught in routine, like a fish in a net, I gasped for breath and no one saw.

The clock is only a cheap plastic thing. I should throw it away and get a new one. After all, that's what you do with broken things, right? But I can't. Suddenly I'm on my knees, searching the tiled floor for a tiny piece of plastic, knowing that each moment that passes is losing me money.

The little hand is nestled neatly in the grout between two tiles. I pick it up carefully and hold it to me, as I once held you. And then I get to my feet and look at the mother hand, as she moves up towards the twelve, where she would normally meet her child. And that's when I know work can wait. I might still catch the bus if I run. I'll mend the clock later, with some glue, but right now, I can hold this child to its mother, for one precious minute. And in that minute I'll remember the time before you were swallowed by a uniform and learned to march to the beat of power and greed. Before your steps were measured by shoe-shined rules. Before they sent you to a country whose name I can't spell or pronounce, to fight for a cause I can't understand or support.

The doorbell is sudden and harsh as a hyena's cry. I'll ignore it. Whoever it is will go away. But they don't. The bell screeches again. I look at my phone. 11.57. I close the kitchen door firmly and move towards the clock, and then there's a knock on the back door. And a face peering through the window.

The face belongs to a head tilted slightly to one side. A woman. Hard to tell her age. She's holding up a pile of leaflets.

I gesture to her to go away. I don't want to buy whatever she's selling. She's saying something. I can't hear through the double glazing, but I'm starting to read desperation in her eyes. 11.58. Behind me, the mother hand continues her patient journey. I take a step towards the window, to explain, somehow, and then I see the face on the leaflets and the word above the face.

A young man. Handsome, like you were, before they cut your hair. And the blood red letters above the face spell Missing. The woman's mouth is framed around a please. 11.59. I'm still holding the little hand firmly, as she once held his hand, as I once held yours.

I open my palm to show her the tiny piece of plastic that nestles there. She stares, fascinated, as time moves on to noon and I step back towards the clock. I reach up and hold the little hand to its parent. Our eyes hold each other and she smiles and holds her arm above her head, as she joins me in this curious ritual only a mother would understand.

I count the seconds with my breath, before I gently remove the little hand from her mother and wrap her in my fingers, and the mother hand continues on her slow, smooth journey. The face at the window watches and smiles. And then I unlock the door and ask how I can help.

On Kings and Falling
Roppotucha Greenberg

So powerful was the king that his death filled up the sky. At high noon, the darkness stood still: it made us think fast and clear, and drink. So jolly was our king, that he hadn't disappeared at all; not him: we all disappeared instead. We exterminated ourselves thoroughly.

By mid-afternoon, we were falling infinitely into nothingness, still clutching post-funeral-drinks and sardines and choking on small talk. Shot glasses were falling beside us, as we argued about the rate of acceleration and the horrible wrong that had been done to the laws of physics and human decency.

As we fell, we grabbed at the walls (leaving greasy marks), at the country, at bits of the evening news. Everything slid down into yogurt eating, cornflake spilling, couch sitting, TV gazing. Into the depths of the couch we flew.

And sometimes we tried to go shopping for shoes, or just to sit in a coffee shop, but it never quite worked. They didn't stock the right shoes, and there weren't any golden coins left. The kingdom was re-mortgaged. Besides there was Geography homework or a book report, and one needed a white shirt for tomorrow's assembly and the iron was missing.

That stuff on the news was confusing. When other people died, in an explosion, or in an abandoned fridge, or if a roof caved in, it suggested unclear comparisons with our own state. We blamed each other for wallowing in the confusingly tragic news.

And there was static on TV after the midnight newsreel. The static never carried messages from outer space and never synched with the buzz of the fridge, or the tiny hurt snores and wheezes.

In the early hours of the morning, our country became known as the country of infinite falling. And just then: thump: we landed. Pale imagoes we were, newly emerged from the discarded pupa of grief. We dripped. We lost all our watches. Crocodiles stomped underneath us.

And a rumour was started that we had to climb along the curved spine of the earth back to his deserted kingdom. We had grown as we fell, and now our lives awaited us.

And another rumour was that he hadn't died at all. He might have assumed the form of a giant ball of fire and was rolling cosily across the warming sky. Or they might have made a mistake, and he was out there, outside, in a black Jaguar, with a bottle of champagne ever-ready, a bouquet of flowers, and a whistle to rouse people in pyjamas and make them look out of the window. Or that we were likely to find him if we used our pickaxes and rope ladders well enough to reach the top of the planet by morning.

So we climbed into the new morning, and the new high noon, and the long unknown hours beyond.

Under the L
by Liam Hogan

'Twelve o'clock?' Emma asked.

'*Noon*, lass. Tomorrow. When the sun is at its highest. That's when you'll meet the love of your life.'

'Outside Primark?'

'Third window from the left.'

Emma stared at the matchmaker's table. It was strewn with almanacs and tarot cards and star charts. A crystal ball covered in a gauzy scarf hadn't, thankfully, been brought into play, but everything else had, from a lengthy perusal of her sweaty palm to waving crystals around on pieces of cotton thread.

'You *sure* about this?'

'Quite,' the matchmaker *slash* fortune teller replied. 'That'll be fifty quid.'

Emma had tried the dating apps. Of course she had, from Tinder to Bumble. But she'd quickly become discouraged. All the men seemed to be lying about something, whether it was their careers, their intentions, or more ridiculously, their height. What; they didn't expect her to notice when they rocked up shorter than Emma's five-nine?

The advert in the newsagent's window had led with: 'Guaranteed Success'. She'd half expected a lengthy questionnaire, a techie crunching the numbers before a computer spat out a name. An *offline* dating agency. Instead, a woman, whose nose and ears betrayed her advanced age, stooped on the basement doorstep at the address listed, peering owlishly through bottle-thick lenses.

'Ah. You're here for a matching.'

Emma flustered. 'Yes... the ad? In Smithys? It said—'

'I've more than one iron in the fire, girl. Come in, come in. You're letting all the heat out.'

'Can't you at least describe my match to me?' Emma asked, fumbling for her purse. Somehow she knew the matchmaker wouldn't take credit cards.

'Doesn't work that way.'

The crone softened. 'Just *be* there. It'll all come good. Promise. Or your money back.'

Emma wondered if, should she ever have the courage to ask for a refund, she'd find the old woman gone. Or maybe she'd belligerently deny having ever promised anything. Or worse, accuse Emma of messing up her one chance of happiness, by not following the crone's exact instructions. Noon, indeed!

Back home, she tackled her younger-by-a-decade brother for astronomical information.

'Sammy,' she asked, all innocent. 'When's noon?'

Sammy looked up from his iPad. Unlike other kids his age, he was probably watching some science lecture or another.

'Well,' he said, thoughtful, 'it's winter, so you don't have to worry about daylight savings. But high noon varies according to your latitude—'

'It does?' Emma interjected, unsure if latitude was the one that went east to west or north-south.

Sammy nodded, solemn. 'Back before the railways, towns used to run to their own local times. Hmm. Tell you what, bring up the weather app for this postcode.'

'O-kay...'

'See the sunrise and sunset times? Split it down the middle and that should give you solar, or meridian, noon.'

'Thanks, geek.'

'De nada, dork.'

Emma kept checking the time on her iPhone. The real problem wasn't the being in the right place at noon. It was the being there at all. The one thing she couldn't, mustn't do, was be seen lurking outside Primark. Her so called friends would never let her forget it.

The third window from the left was occupied by a huge red poster. Not yet Christmas and already the sales had begun. She wavered, stood by the M&S food hall on the other side. She'd done Sammy's trick with the times, was waiting until the last minute before crossing the road. But what if she'd got it wrong? Maybe she should've asked her brother to calculate it? But then he'd want to know why, and... oh, it didn't bear telling. Fifty quid, for this!

She craned her head to look up at the pale blue sky. The sun was around, somewhere, but her side of the street was deep in shadow, and the low angle of the sun cast that shadow all the way to the other, Primark side.

Reluctantly she crossed, stood under the L of 'SALE'. She kept squinting up at the rooftops of the buildings opposite. Still couldn't see the sun, but the dazzle around the chimney pots told her it was up there.

And then, like clouds parting, a shaft of light snuck between two of the chimney stacks, falling directly on her like a spotlight in a theatre.

'You too, hey?' said a soft, Irish lilt beside her. Her dazzled eyes struggled to make out the speaker. Red hair, freckles. Wearing sunglasses, as if prepared for this moment.

'Me too *what*?' Had this girl been to the fortune teller as well? Were they both there, waiting for the same bloody guy? The same *perfect match*? If so, Emma was going to do more than ask for a refund. She'd tear the old crone apart. It was made worse that her 'competitor' was so undeniably cute.

'The sun, only hitting this spot on one day a year, on the solstice, exactly at noon. *That* what,' the girl replied, a whimsical smile in the sparkling light.

Emma almost nodded her head. As if this was carefully planned. But then she thought about all those untruths on the dating sites. 'I didn't know,' she admitted. 'I mean, I knew it was noon and the solstice, but... not this. I guess I'm here mostly by chance.'

An arm snaked through hers. 'Lucky you. I'm Alice.'

When the fortune teller wandered past on the other side of the road, long after the sun had continued on its way, dipping the SALE sign back into shadow, neither girl noticed, too engrossed in conversation. A conversation that would last for a further two hours over lunch in a pub Alice knew, tucked away from the Christmas shopping frenzy, and then be picked up the evening after, at a wine bar Emma chose.

The crone nodded in satisfaction, and gave herself five stars on Yelp.

Noon Child Unknown
Diana Powell

There was something about – not going out – in the midday sun.

Scraps of words from an old rhyme – or was it a song? – drifted deep in her mind, calling 'Lena, Lena,' but she couldn't catch them, or put them back together.

Still, it made sense, didn't it? It was the hottest part of the day, the sun highest in the sky. Too warm for children to play tag through the Stones, too breathless for gathering wild flowers at the edge of the Circle, too hot for anything, anyone.

'Yes, the Old Wives whispered tales, sitting by their hearths, leaning close,' her mother told her.

'Saying things to stop us doing what we shouldn't. Turning the hermit in the hut on the banks of the river into a troll who lurked beneath the uncertain bridge. Magicking the cave on the mountain, too high for climbing, into the lair of the dragon, a fire-breathing monster! We believed it all, then; until older, we knew none of it for truth.'

For children, intent on staying outside when white shafts from the sky bore down into small, thin skulls, when red heat addled their weak blood and minds, there was a witch who appeared, and took them away. A white lady ('there's always a white lady!'); or a wizened hag ('there's always a wizened hag!'); or, sometimes, a young maiden, roaming the field bounds. Took them away, cut off their heads, or left them mad; if they didn't stay indoors.

But it was just a tale. And *she* didn't have a child, did she?

It wasn't summer now. The earth had turned exactly half way round. A semi-circle, a twist of a giant's hand, or a god's, she supposed. Summer solstice, winter solstice. High sun, low sun, hot, cold. A turn-about, an opposite to that day, when–

The Wise Men told her, no, it wasn't 'exact' at all. They spoke of solar noons and altitudes and lines drawn on the earth; the angle of the sun. No giants, or gods, just 'science'.

They knew more than her.

Others always knew more than her.

'Since yesterday,' they said, 'our 'twenty-four hours' has gained thirty-six seconds. Twenty-three more than in the summer.'

'Look at your shadow,' they told her. 'See how much longer it is. The longest of any time in the year.'

'Wait!'

'Now…!'

'Now' was the first of the bells, one! – silencing the chatter with their noise, clamouring the thoughts in her head, demanding that 'Now' turned into 'Then'. Two, three… until twelve lingered in the air, holding their breath tight, stopping their limbs. That was when the Lady appeared – on the last strike. Stroke of the bell, struck by the sun. Strike of the devil woman. The dust clouds were the first sign, louring in the distance, whirling closer, entering their gaping mouths, cloying their lungs. Then they saw it, the figure dancing through them; saw the scythe in her hands, flailing from side to side. The men shouted, waving, calling. The mothers took their children's hands and ran. Only she stayed where she was, in the centre of the Circle, arms raised to the midday sun – there was no need for *her* to run. Was there?

Now, she wishes she'd listened to the men, the Old Wives – anyone– then, just as she listens to them now.

One, two… twenty-two, twenty-three. Holly-berry, mistletoe, holly-berry, mistletoe; counting out the words, holding them in her hand. Twenty-three blinks of an eye, just enough, perhaps. Enough for a head start, perhaps, away from the demon. Or enough to pause for a while, along the way, to get her breath back, to give her the strength to go on again.

And if she had *this* – what she sees in front of her – if she had been this figure stretching away from her, so tall and thin, with such long legs – how much faster her gait would have been! A vault over the scattered stones, a jump over the fallen trees through the nearby wood, enough to leave the noon-witch behind.

Any of these things might have made a difference. Any of them could have saved the child-unknown she carried deep inside.

There are no witches for the winter solstice, as far as she knows. It makes no difference anyway. There is no heat. So there is no falling to the floor. No pain. No bleeding. There is no new child to steal. There will never be another, they tell her.

Gone, gone with the midday witch, last summer, Lady Noon.

All there is now is a feeble sun low in the sky. And a long, such a long shadow, cast in front of her.

Up on the Roof
Lily Peters

The alarm rings at quarter to. Work starts at noon. At noon, the winds are at their strongest and the sun at its highest although that would be hard to tell. Up on the roof, the cloud is so thick, you can almost eat it. It has been a year and a half since I have seen blue sky.

It is an uncomfortable feeling, being shrouded in clouds. The sky seems heavier than the ground. Gravity seems confused too, and the ground trembles every other day or so. The mantle of the earth is trying its damnedest to shake us off, and into the clouds.

I don't blame it.

I roll out of my cot. Standing too quickly, I bang my head. The narrow rooms where we now live are as oppressive as the clouds. The plaster smells constantly of damp. I've learnt it is best to put my uniform on last thing, so as to keep the dank smell at bay.

I have time to spare. I close my eyes against the grey hum of the single energy-saving bulb, it does funny things to my vision. I often see shadows when trying to sleep, I can almost make out words scrawled beneath the ever-damp paint above my cot.

Sometimes, I consider adding to the historic document, but I don't know where there are any pens. Also, I have more or less forgotten how to write.

And, what would I say?

Before Everything Went Wrong, time to spare had been a luxury. Five minutes meant a status update, a few picture-flicks to spy on friends or past lovers. A chat with a parent, a quickly scribbled birthday card.

Now there are no phones. No-one I know. No parents. No birthdays.

I decide to be early. Maybe whoever cares about these things will notice. Maybe I'll be promoted. To what, I'm not sure. The hierarchy is still unclear to me. Perhaps this is because it needs to be.

Five to.
My cubicle door shuts slowly behind me. I start to climb the twelve flights to the roof.
I make myself recount what was before. It does get easier, the more I relive the moments.
A moment for every flight of stair:

One: Snatches of blue sky in a summer heatwave, some years ago. Snatches of headlines predicting environmental doom.

Two: Our dogs panting heavily, overheating. September, October – no need for coats when we walked them in November.

Three: Dogs starving now, bones sticking out everywhere. No reason, said the vet – perhaps something in their food? Something in the air?
I wipe some sweat from my cheek. The gun clinks against my left leg. Where is that vet now?

Four: Unnatural, midday darkness. Silent birds. Silent people, hurrying in the streets. Supermarkets empty of the milk that was already starting to taste sour.
Here, there isn't any food as such, just nutrient mulch. It is a similar colour to the walls and the clouds. A pallid margin laps at everything here. It is not as tragic as you might think, not having windows. There is nothing outside to see.

Five: Sleeping with the bedroom windows open on Christmas Eve – sheets sticking to us in the heat.

I lick some sweat from my top lip and keep a steady pace. Climbing up and up.

Six: New Year's Day – the dead birds all over the ground. The moans as the smell began to rise.

I am almost at the roof now. Almost ready to keep watch.

Seven: Thick air choking us as we moved to the bunker. Or were moved. People in masks, silent, unforgivingly uninformative. Holding guns.

Guns like the one I hold now.

Eight: The sadness of the bunker. Beds everywhere, bodies supine, eyes glued to the grey ceiling.

Nine: The protection of the bunker. The comforting whir of the air conditioning.

A whine of irony at its continued use, even at the planet's end.

Two minutes to go and I am at the door to the roof. I lean against it for just a moment. It is difficult for me to catch my breath these days.

Ten: The questions that haunted the waking minutes. Where were the dogs now? Were they alive? Was the house on fire, looted? Gone? Hushed conversations between beds, and the dawning realisation that everything we once knew had been twisted. All had been heated and cooled, and was now unrecognisable.

Eleven: Your hand, when it stopped squeezing.

Twelve: Stepping out alone when they opened the bunker. The new, grey sky.

I hurl myself against the door and fall out onto the roof. High railings loom over me. Feeling dizzy, I crouch for a moment, letting this depleted world spin around me.
I wipe my cheek again and shoulder my gun. I stand, I look up – hoping to see a flying shape amongst the clouds.

I gasp.
It is noon.
The sky is blue.

ABOUT THE AUTHORS

With so many authors involved, including biographical notes here would tip the book into another section of sixteen pages. You can find details of *all* our authors and poets on our website: www.arachnepress.com.

ABOUT ARACHNE PRESS

Arachne Press is a micro-publisher of (award-winning!) short story and poetry anthologies and collections, novels, including a Carnegie Medal nominated young adult novel, and a photographic portrait collection.
We are expanding our range all the time, but the short form is our first love. We keep fiction and poetry live, through readings, the Solstice Shorts Festival, workshops, exhibitions and all things to do with writing.

Follow us on Twitter:
@ArachnePress
@SolShorts

Like us on Facebook:
ArachnePress
SolsticeShorts2014

The Solstice Shorts Festival
(http://arachnepress.com/solstice-shorts)
Now into its fifth year, Solstice Shorts is all about time: held on the shortest day of the year on the Prime meridian, (and elsewhere) stories, poetry and song celebrate the turning of the moon, the changing of the seasons, the motions of the spheres, and clockwork! Videos of the performances are available on our website and on the Solstice Shorts Facebook page: SolsticeShorts2014
Next themes: 2019 *Time and Tide,* and 2020, *Dawn*... get writing!

We are always on the lookout for other places to show off, so if you run a bookshop, a literature festival or any other kind of literature venue, get in touch; we'd love to talk to you.

Workshops

We offer occasional writing workshops suitable for writers' groups, literature festivals and evening classes, which are sometimes supported by live music – if you are interested, please get in touch.

OTHER SOLSTICE SHORTS BOOKS

Solstice Shorts: Sixteen Stories about Time
ISBN: 978-1-909208-23-0 £9.99 ANTHOLOGY
Winning stories that chart the meaning of time, exploring what it can do to us, and for us, from the first Solstice Shorts Festival competition plus stories from judges Alison Moore, Imogen Robertson, Robert Shearman, and Anita Sethi.

Shortest Day, Longest Night: Poems & Stories from the Solstice Shorts Festival 2015 & 2016
ISBN 978-1-909208-28-5 £9.99 ANTHOLOGY
Celebrating the shortest day of the year, which is also short story day, with stories, poems and songs to an appropriate theme. 23 stories and 34 poems featuring old gods, bitter weather, darkness, light, neighbourliness, looping days, birth, death and if not the *meaning* of the universe, *possibly* the end of it.

DUSK: Stories and poems from Solstice Shorts Festival 2017

ISBN 978-1-909208-54-4 £9.99 ANTHOLOGY
On 21st December 2017, the shortest day of the year, 18 stories and 28 poems celebrating DUSK were read live on 12 sites, from pubs to woodlands, in a wave of words across the UK.

Other Anthologies

Liberty Tales: Stories and Poems inspired by Magna Carta
ISBN 978-1-909208-31-5 £9.99 ANTHOLOGY
Liberty, personal and legal, is the starting point of this wide ranging collection of responses to the Magna Carta, some directly relating to specific clauses of the document signed by King John, others more concerned with how we experience and search after freedom in the 21st Century, because Freedom never goes out of fashion.

Five by Five
ISBN FICTION £9.99 ANTHOLOGY (Fiction)
A showcase for authors we have published previously in anthologies, giving a wider perspective on their writing. Cassandra Passarelli, Katy Darby, Joan Taylor-Rowan, Sarah James, Helen Morris.

We/She
ISBN 978-1-909208-62-9 £9.99 ANTHOLOGY (fiction)
In collaboration with Liars' League.
A celebration of the centenary of women in the UK getting the vote. Stories by women, performed at one of Liars' League's events in London, Hong Kong or New York.

Vindication

ISBN 978-1-909208-65-0 £9.99 ANTHOLOGY (Poetry)
A showcase for poets we have published singly in anthologies, giving a wider perspective on their writing. Sarah James, Elinor Brooks, Jill Sharp, Sarah Lawson, Anne Macaulay and Adrienne Silcock.

The Other Side of Sleep: Narrative Poems
ISBN: 978-1-909208-18-6 ~~£9.99~~ £5.00
ANTHOLOGY (Poetry)
Long, narrative poems by contemporary voices, including Inua Elams, Brian Johnstone, and Kate Foley, whose title poem for the anthology was the winner of the 2014 Second Light Long Poem competition.

London Lies ISBN: 978-1-909208-00-1 ~~£9.99~~ **£5**
ANTHOLOGY (Fiction)
Our first Liars' League showcase, featuring unlikely tales set in London.

Stations: Short Stories Inspired by the Overground Line
ISBN: 978-1-909208-01-8 ~~£10.99~~ **£5** ANTHOLOGY (Fiction)
A story for every station from New Cross, Crystal Palace, and West Croydon at the Southern extremes of the East London line all the way to Highbury & Islington.

Lovers' Lies ISBN: 978-1-909208-02-5 ~~£9.99~~ **£5**
ANTHOLOGY (Fiction)
Our second collaboration with Liars' League, bringing the freshness, wit, imagination and passion of their authors to stories of love.

Weird Lies ISBN: 978-1-909208-10-0 ~~£9.99~~ **£5**
ANTHOLOGY (SF/Fantasy Fiction)
WINNER of the Saboteur2014 Best Anthology Award. Our third Liars' League collaboration – more than twenty stories varying in style from tales not out of place in One Thousand and One Nights to the completely bemusing.

Order Direct
from **our webshop** at
https://arachnepress.com/shop/
or from **Inpress**
www.inpressbooks.co.uk
or your local book shop or online retailer.
All our books, apart from poetry collections, are also available as ebooks from your usual provider.